Learning Cursive
with the
Founding Fathers

TRANSCRIBING AMERICAN HISTORY FROM
THE ORIGINAL DOCUMENTS AND
HANDWRITTEN LETTERS.
READING AND WRITING CURRICULUM
WORKBOOK FOR HOMESCHOOLERS.

PUSH BACK PRESS

Table of Contents

Why primary sources?

A primary source is an original source of information that we can use to study any question or issue we are interested in. Such documents consist of materials presented by the actual author or eyewitnesses rather than interpretations or analyses based on other people's opinions. Any artifact that provides a first-hand account of an event, object, person, or work of art can serve as a primary source. It could be could be an official government document, a personal letter, a piece of art and more. Because they reflect personal observations, such historical items enable us to get closer to the past and see for ourselves exactly what happened, as well as what people of the time felt and thought about it.

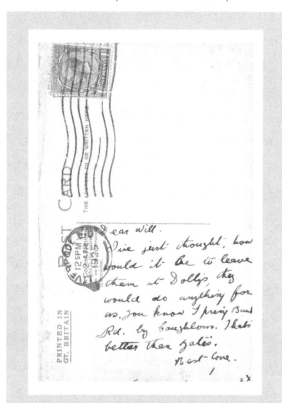

In contrast, Secondary sources are indirect accounts of the event or person of the research. Textbooks, fictional books and state-commissioned propaganda are examples of historical materials written by "experts" or other motivated persons who wish to contribute to human knowledge of history. Although secondary sources can be useful, providing facts, context, and background information, they can't offer the same level of detail as primary sources do. Today, powerful forces in our world are dedicated to rewriting Western history and civilization. They paint a false picture of our past, values and culture. So, while we don't dismiss secondary sources, we should never be left entirely dependent on other people's opinions and

Before emails and Social Media, people used to keep in touch through personal correspondence, like letters and post cards.

prejudices. Instead, we must know how to read the original letters, diaries, and documents ourselves. This way, we can make up our own minds based on what we read with our own eyes. This is the best way to protect ourselves from deception.

Keeping all that in mind, the further back in time we go, we find that more and more primary sources were written by hand, in cursive. This is why it is so important not only to write cursive but also to learn how to read different penmanship styles written by various authors. This would prepare us to study any primary source we wish to examine.

So, what's cursive anyway?

Cursive is a form of writing by hand in which the writer uses flowing, joined strokes to produce single letters or words while lifting the pen off the paper as little as possible. Cursive writing is not only more beautiful than block print letters, but it also can be quicker to write. The Founding Fathers wrote in various styles, including print and cursive. While some were known for their elegant handwriting, others were not. In this book, you'll have the opportunity to play with different cursive fonts as you read different penmanship styles. We'll study original letters from Benjamin Franklin, George Washington, Thomas Jefferson, Frederick Douglass, and Abraham Lincoln. This will allow you to try them all so you can develop your own personal cursive style and signature.

Today, most writing is done on a computer keyboard, not paper. So, why would handwriting be necessary for our digital age? Consider the following. Many politicians and bureaucrats in charge of American education might think of cursive as an archaic, useless skill. Others, who have a private plan for changing our culture by changing our national history, may find it convenient for students to lose the ability to read the founding documents. Such people may think it good luck that students remain reliant on state-approved secondary sources, filled with politically correct interpretations and opinions that won't be discovered as propaganda. For such administrators, the loss of handwriting skills is a blessing. Did you know Common Core standards that govern teaching in American public schools don't include any requirements for handwriting instruction?

Cursive reading skills can be incredibly helpful, allowing us to take an authentic glimpse into the original thoughts and opinions and gain more meaningful knowledge of history. This can be the greatest advantage if we want to grow our understanding of where we come from, where we are heading, and what steps to take to correct the course of our destiny.

THE CURSIVE ALPHABET

A = $\mathcal{A}$	a = a	N = $\mathcal{N}$	n = n
B = $\mathcal{B}$	b = b	O = $\mathcal{O}$	o = o
C = $\mathcal{C}$	c = c	P = $\mathcal{P}$	p = p
D = $\mathcal{D}$	d = d	Q = $\mathcal{Q}$	q = q
E = $\mathcal{E}$	e = e	R = $\mathcal{R}$	r = r
F = $\mathcal{F}$	f = f	S = $\mathcal{S}$	s = s
G = $\mathcal{G}$	g = g	T = $\mathcal{T}$	t = t
H = $\mathcal{H}$	h = h	U = $\mathcal{U}$	u = u
I = $\mathcal{I}$	i = i	V = $\mathcal{V}$	v = v
J = $\mathcal{J}$	j = j	W = $\mathcal{W}$	w = w
K = $\mathcal{K}$	k = k	X = $\mathcal{X}$	x = x
L = $\mathcal{L}$	l = l	Y = $\mathcal{Y}$	y = y
M = $\mathcal{M}$	m = m	Z = $\mathcal{Z}$	z = z

Trace over and practice the cursive letter A.

Trace over and practice the cursive letter A.

$\mathscr{A}$ $\mathscr{A}$ $\mathscr{A}$

$\mathscr{A}$ $\mathscr{A}$

$\mathscr{A}$

$\mathscr{A}$

$\mathscr{A}$

a a a

a a

Each lower case cursive letter has a front and a back tail, which enables it to be naturally connected to the previous and the following letters. On the words listed below, notice how the connecting tails permit the smooth blending of the letters. Practice merging neighboring letters within a word whenever possible by tracing over each word without lifting your pen or pencil except where absolutely necessary (for example, when crossing the letters "A" or "t".)

Anna Anthony April apple anatomy

Alabama Albania Ariel banana sap

Trace over and practice the cursive letter B.

Trace over and practice the cursive letter B.

B B B

B B

B

B

B

b b b

b b

b

b

b

Bombay Bambi bomb bon-bon bamboo bit byte best

Barbara Babylon Ben book babbling boy broom bic

Trace over and practice the cursive letter C.

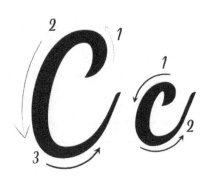
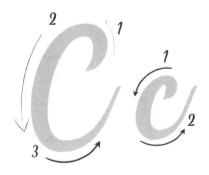

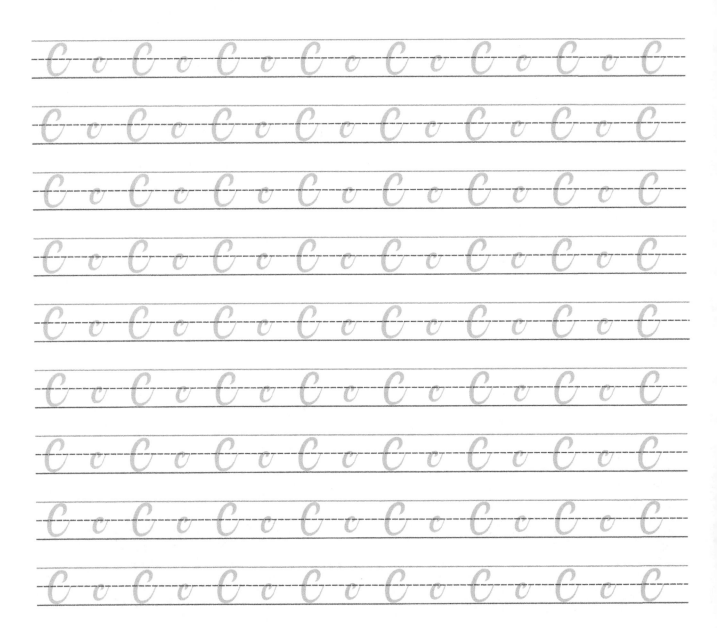

Trace over and practice the cursive letter C.

C C C

C C

C

C

C

c c c

c c

c

c

c

Cancun Canada Coca-Cola coconut cocoon doc

Cody Carolina can cook account cat act accept

Trace over and practice the cursive letter D.

Trace over and practice the cursive letter D.

D D D

D D

D

D

D

d d d

d d

d

d

d

Dubai Denmark ditch dent dedication noodle middle mad

Daddy Dundee Danube Dan day deer dog dodo desk

Trace over and practice the cursive letter E.

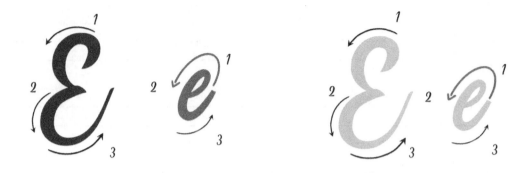

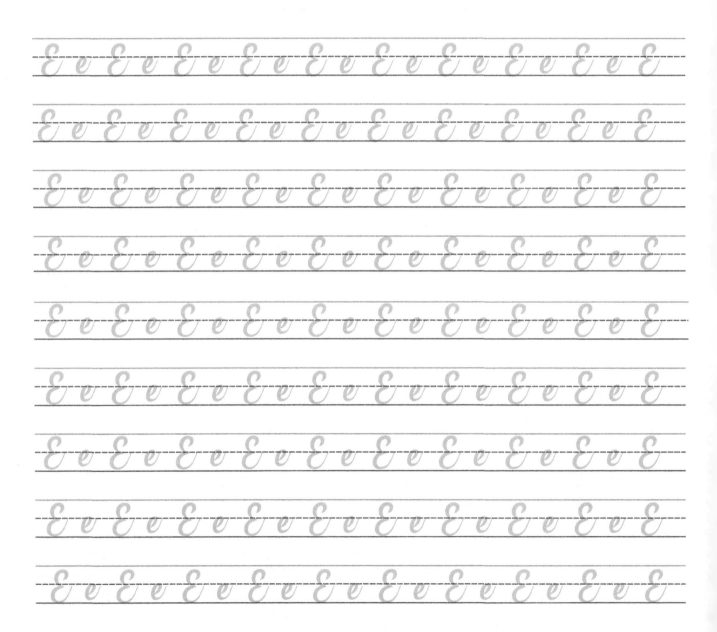

Trace over and practice the cursive letter E.

E E E

E E

E

E

E

e e e

e e

e

e

e

Eleonore Evelyn Eve envelope elk metal we

Ecuador Ella Elon developer deer meet rod

Trace over and practice the cursive letter F.

Trace over and practice the cursive letter F.

F F F

F F

F

F

F

f f f

f f

f

f

f

France Frankfurt of if office face off roof for buff

Frank Ford Fred fluff fob beef fate fake fifty fox

Trace over and practice the cursive letter G.

Trace over and practice the cursive letter G.

$\mathcal{G}$ $\mathcal{G}$ $\mathcal{G}$

$\mathcal{G}$ $\mathcal{G}$

$\mathcal{G}$

$\mathcal{G}$

$\mathcal{G}$

g g g

g g

g

g

g

Germany George go bugging bag fog gag muggle great

Gregory Gaga Google leggings rouge sagging baggage egg

Trace over and practice the cursive letter H.

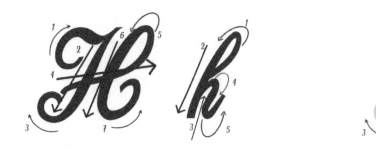

Trace over and practice the cursive letter H.

H H H

H H

H

H

H

h h h

h h

h

h

h

Honolulu Helsinki Holland has him ha-ha hello hit

Hanna Honda Hanover hand hot heat them hat hop

Trace over and practice the cursive letter I.

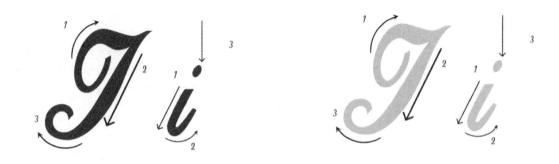

Trace over and practice the cursive letter I.

$\mathcal{I}$ $\mathcal{I}$ $\mathcal{I}$

$\mathcal{I}$ $\mathcal{I}$

$\mathcal{I}$

$\mathcal{I}$

$\mathcal{I}$

i i i

i i

i

i

i

Iran Ivan Iris Issac Icarus if in mini big rig fig

Ives Iraq Idaho mill kick sick nick rich big ibis mic

Trace over and practice the cursive letter J.

Trace over and practice the cursive letter J.

$\mathcal{J}$ $\mathcal{J}$ $\mathcal{J}$

$\mathcal{J}$ $\mathcal{J}$

$\mathcal{J}$

$\mathcal{J}$

$\mathcal{J}$

j j j

j j

j

j

j

John Jack Julie Johannesburg Jacob juice jinni job jade

Judy June July Joan January Jewish Jedi jab judo

Trace over and practice the cursive letter K.

Trace over and practice the cursive letter K.

$\mathcal{K}$ $\mathcal{K}$ $\mathcal{K}$

$\mathcal{K}$ $\mathcal{K}$

$\mathcal{K}$

$\mathcal{K}$

$\mathcal{K}$

k k k

k k

k

k

k

Korea Kenya kabuki khaki kite book back duck kit

Ken Kabul Kathrine kale clock sack neck back

Trace over and practice the cursive letter L.

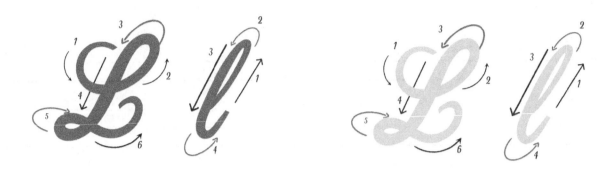

Trace over and practice the cursive letter L.

L L L

L L

L

L

L

l l l

l l

l

l l

l l

Lilly Leila Libya La-la Land ball salt let lilac lip

Lebanon Lucy lake doll lavender love life ill lolly lore

Trace over and practice the cursive letter M.

Trace over and practice the cursive letter M.

M M M

M M

M

M

M

m m m

m m

m

m

m

Monaco Montana Mini-Me mammal map comma

Miami Miriam Mimi May Monday mammoth

Trace over and practice the cursive letter N.

Trace over and practice the cursive letter N.

N N N

N N

N

N

N

n n n

n n

n

n

n

Netherlands North Carolina not inside gone and cannot rein

Saint Nick Nina cannon net nano inning new mini

Trace over and practice the cursive letter O.

Trace over and practice the cursive letter O.

𝒪 𝒪 𝒪

𝒪 𝒪

𝒪

𝒪

𝒪

𝑜 𝑜 𝑜

𝑜 𝑜

𝑜

𝑜

𝑜

Oslo Ontario oblong boy boot book baboon mock oh root

Otto Ohio Olga to on of vote robot octagon for soap

Trace over and practice the cursive letter P.

Trace over and practice the cursive letter P.

P P P

P P

P

P

P

p p p

p p

p

p

p

Popper Paul paper pepper pot proper pet copper

Poland Peter pomp pest poke penny pop supper

Trace over and practice the cursive letter Q.

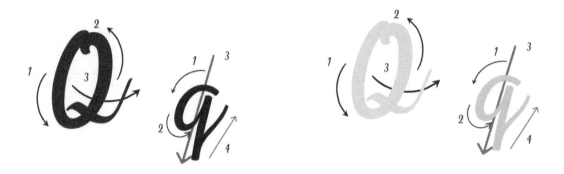

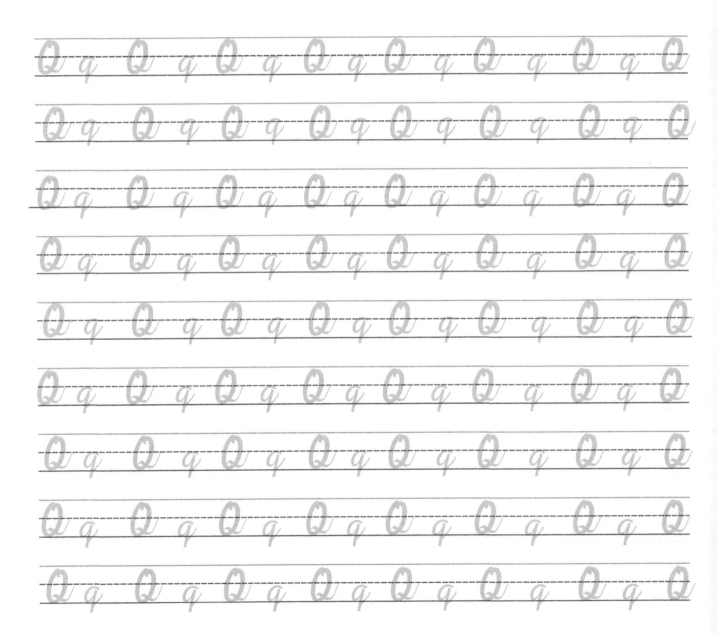

Trace over and practice the cursive letter Q.

Q   Q   Q

Q   Q

Q

Q

Q

q   q   q

q   q

q

q

q

Qatar   quote   quick   etiquette   opaque   quadrant

Queen squad   question   quantity   quit   quite   query

Trace over and practice the cursive letter R.

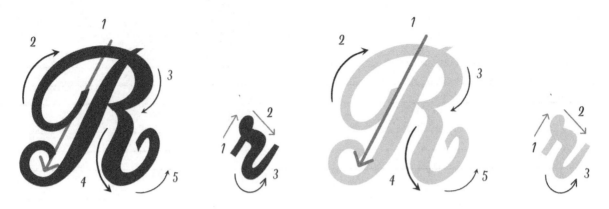

Trace over and practice the cursive letter R.

R R R

R R

R

R

R

r r r

r r

r

r

r

Rome Rotterdam or barring roar report core board

Russia Ron Robespierre rare room oar rat red rare

Trace over and practice the cursive letter S.

Trace over and practice the cursive letter S.

$\mathcal{S}$ $\mathcal{S}$ $\mathcal{S}$

$\mathcal{S}$ $\mathcal{S}$

$\mathcal{S}$

$\mathcal{S}$

$\mathcal{S}$

s s s

s s

s

s

s

Samsung Susan Sussex has mass shoe boss is gloss

Santa Sasquatch Sam Ross sassy set mess as pest

Trace over and practice the cursive letter T.

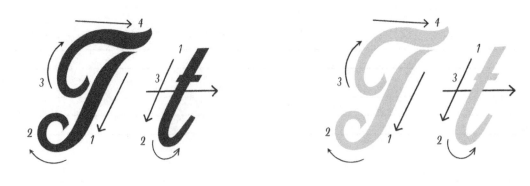

Trace over and practice the cursive letter T.

$\mathcal{T}$ $\mathcal{T}$ $\mathcal{T}$

$\mathcal{T}$ $\mathcal{T}$

$\mathcal{T}$

$\mathcal{T}$

$\mathcal{T}$

t t t

t t

t

t

t

Tony Tatum total not that with tainted mat butter cot

Tom Timothy Titanic tattoo tatter bat totem it tote sat

Trace over and practice the cursive letter U.

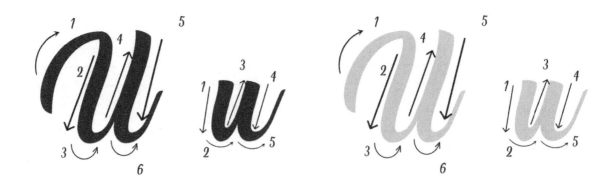

Trace over and practice the cursive letter U.

U U U

U U

U

U

U

u u u

u u

u

u

u

Uruguay Urdu under umbrella butter route que

Uganda Uber Luna cute tune muumuu muse

Trace over and practice the cursive letter V.

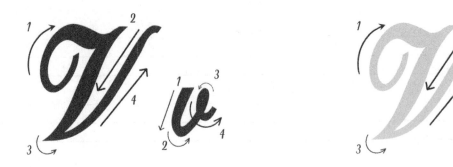

Trace over and practice the cursive letter V.

$\mathcal{V}$ $\mathcal{V}$ $\mathcal{V}$

$\mathcal{V}$ $\mathcal{V}$

$\mathcal{V}$

$\mathcal{V}$

$\mathcal{V}$

v v v

v v

v

v

v

Vivian Vienna Victor vivacious vine eve vibe view cove

Venezuela Vicky every vet violin visit vanilla vain viper

Trace over and practice the cursive letter W.

Trace over and practice the cursive letter W.

W W W

W W

W

W

W

w w w

w w

w

w

w

West Will Wanda we witness ware wait win was

Willow Wales wake window wind well wet wake

Trace over and practice the cursive letter X.

Trace over and practice the cursive letter X.

X X X

X X

X

X

X

x x x

x x

x

x

x

Xerox X-ray Texas Mexico Rex fix six ox box

Xenia Xerxes extra extension exit exercise express next

Trace over and practice the cursive letter Y.

Trace over and practice the cursive letter Y.

Y Y Y

Y Y

Y

Y

Y

y y y

y y

y

y

y

Yemen York yes yet by my many yolk byte yams

Yankee yoga yacht yesterday day yellow coyote yo-yo

Trace over and practice the cursive letter Z.

Trace over and practice the cursive letter Z.

Z   Z   Z

Z   Z

Z

Z

Z

z   z   z

z   z

z

z

z

Zaire   Zach   Zoom   zipper   zelot   zero   bizarre

Zanzibar   Zoolander   zephyr   zebra   zit   zenith

Primary Source

1.

Petition to King George III
October 25, 1774

PETITION TO KING GEORGE III
October 25, 1774.

By the late 18th century, after several expensive wars fought on the American continent, England's debt doubled. So naturally, the Crown sought to recover some of these expenses by raising new taxes in the colonies. As far as the British were concerned, they had protected the colonists at a huge cost, and now it was time to recover their investment.

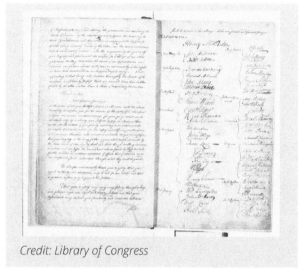

Credit: Library of Congress

However, the American colonists didn't see it this way. They didn't have any representation in the English Parliament. So, from their point of view, it wasn't appropriate to be treated as regular English citizens. That's what the Boston Tea Party was about. Not that tea became very expensive all of a sudden. No, the problem, according to Bostonians, was "taxation without representation", they were taxed by the Crown, yet, they had no voice in their own country's governance.

After the Boston Tea Party, the British were very upset about the open rebellion. In response, the Parliament retaliated with the Coercive Acts of 1774. The new laws were so cruel and unfair that community leaders from the colonies got together and, under the authority of the Continental Congress, wrote a petition to King George III. The idea was first to appease him and improve the relationship between the home country and the American colonies, but also to address the unfairness of the Coercive Acts.

A Congressional committee was formed and charged with the job of composing a respectful yet clear redress of the American colonists' grievances. Led by their chairman Richard Henry Lee, the rest of the committee members were John Adams, Patrick Henry, Thomas Johnson, and John Rutledge. Unfortunately, we are unsure which of them, or their secretaries penned the final draft that Benjamin Franklin presented to the King.

Regardless of whose beautiful handwriting we read in the letter, this primary source is an authentic piece of the legacy left to us by our Founding Fathers. The Petition to King George III, from October 25, 1774, is a faithful historical record of the initiation of America's conception. The colonists' motivations for fighting and ultimately winning independence are revealed in official papers such as this one and personal letters from that time. It's hard to imagine a better source, a more detailed and comprehensive document to study when considering the major players, events, facts and emotions surrounding the birth of our nation. The primary source we'll examine in the following pages is the first opening page of the Petition. The copy of the document that we are about to consider is preserved in the Library of Congress, in the Benjamin Franklin Papers. The full reference to this and all other primary sources we'll examine can be found at the back of the book.

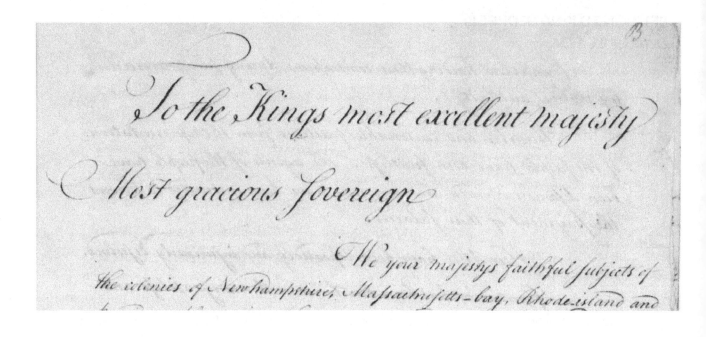

To the Kings most excellent majesty

Most gracious Sovereign

We your majestys faithful subjects of the colonies of

Newhampshire, Massachusetts - bay, Rhode - island and

Transcribe the cursive letters from the opening of the petition to the King:

To   *the*   *Kings*   *most*   *excellent*

| T | o |

| t | h | e |

majesty   *Most*   *gracious*

Sovereign

Transcribe the cursive letters:

We your majestys faithful

☐☐ ☐☐☐☐ ☐☐☐☐☐☐☐ ☐☐☐☐☐☐☐☐

subjects of the colonies of

☐☐☐☐☐☐☐☐ ☐☐ ☐☐☐ ☐☐☐☐☐☐☐ ☐☐

Newhampshire , Massachusetts -

☐☐☐☐☐☐☐☐☐☐☐☐☐ ☐☐☐☐☐☐☐☐☐☐☐☐☐

bay , Rhode – island and

☐☐☐ ☐☐☐☐☐ ☐☐☐☐☐☐ ☐☐☐

Copy in cursive the above excerpt from the petition to the King.

_____

_____

_____

_____

_____

_____

DECODING CURSIVE LEGEND

Aa	*Bb*	*Cc*	*Dd*	*Ee*	*Ff*	*Gg*	*Hh*	*Ii*	*Jj*	*Kk*	*Ll*	*Mm*
Aa	Bb	Cc	Dd	Ee	Ff	Gg	Hh	Ii	Jj	Kk	Ll	Mm
Nn	*Oo*	*Pp*	*Qq*	*Rr*	*Ss*	*Tt*	*Uu*	*Vv*	*Ww*	*Xx*	*Yy*	*Zz*
Nn	Oo	Pp	Qq	Rr	Ss	Tt	Uu	Vv	Ww	Xx	Yy	Zz

providence plantations, Connecticut, New-York, New-Jersey, Pennsylvania, The counties of New-Castle, Kent and Sussex on Delaware, Maryland Virginia, North-Carolina and South Carolina in behalf of ourselves

providence plantation, Connecticut, New-york, New-jersey, Pennsylvania, the counties of New-Castle, Kent and Sussex on Delaware, Maryland, Virginia, North-Carolina and South-Carolina in behalf of ourselves

Transcribe the cursive letters in the excerpt from the petition to the King:

providence   plantation ,

Connecticut ,   New - york ,   New -

jersey ,   Pennsylvania ,   the

counties   of   New -Castle ,   Kent

and   Sussex   on   Delaware ,

Transcribe the cursive letters:

Maryland □□□□□□□□

Virginia , □□□□□□□□

North □□□□□

Carolina □□□□□□□□

and □□□

South □□□□□

Carolina □□□□□□□□

in □□

behalf □□□□□□

of □□

ourselves □□□□□□□□□

Copy in cursive the above excerpt from the petition to the King.

_____

_____

_____

_____

_____

_____

DECODING CURSIVE LEGEND

Aa	*Bb*	*Cc*	*Dd*	*Ee*	*Ff*	*Gg*	*Hh*	*Ii*	*Jj*	*Kk*	*Ll*	*Mm*
Aa	Bb	Cc	Dd	Ee	Ff	Gg	Hh	Ii	Jj	Kk	Ll	Mm
Nn	*Oo*	*Pp*	*Qq*	*Rr*	*Ss*	*Tt*	*Uu*	*Vv*	*Ww*	*Xx*	*Yy*	*Zz*
Nn	Oo	Pp	Qq	Rr	Ss	Tt	Uu	Vv	Ww	Xx	Yy	Zz

and the inhabitants of those colonies who have deputed us to represent them in General Congress, by this our humble petition, beg leave to lay our grievances before the throne.

and the inhabitants of those colonies who have deputed us to represent them in General Congress, by this our humble petition beg leave to lay our grievances before the throne.

Transcribe the cursive letters in the excerpt from the petition to the King:

and the inhabitants of these

colonies who have deputed us

to represent them in General

Congress , by this our humble

petition beg leave to lay our

grievances before the throne .

Try reading a different cursive style.

To the Kings most excellent majesty

Most gracious Sovereign, We your majestys faithful subjects of the colonies of Newhampshire, Massachusetts - bay, Rhode - island and providence plantation, Connecticut, New - york, New - jersey, Pennsylvania, the counties of New - Castle, Kent and Sussex on Delaware, Maryland, Virginia, North - Carolina and South - Carolina in behalf of ourselves and the inhabitants of those colonies who have deputed us to represent them in General Congress, by this our humble petition beg leave to lay our grievances before the throne.

Copy in cursive the above excerpt from the petition to the King.

_____

_____

_____

_____

_____

_____

_____

_____

_____

A standing army has been kept in these colonies, ever since the conclusion of the late war, without the consent of our assemblies; and this army with a considerable naval armament has been employed to enforce the collection of taxes .

A standing army has been kept in these colonies, ever since the conclusion of the late war, without the consent of our assemblies; and this army with a considerable naval armament has been employed to enforce the collection of taxes

Transcribe the cursive letters:

A standing army has been kept

☐ ☐☐☐☐☐☐☐☐ ☐☐☐☐ ☐☐☐ ☐☐☐☐ ☐☐☐☐

in these colonies , ever since

☐☐ ☐☐☐☐☐ ☐☐☐☐☐☐☐☐ ☐☐☐☐ ☐☐☐☐☐

the conclusion of the late

☐☐☐ ☐☐☐☐☐☐☐☐☐☐ ☐☐ ☐☐☐ ☐☐☐☐

war , without the consent of

☐☐☐ ☐☐☐☐☐☐☐ ☐☐☐ ☐☐☐☐☐☐☐ ☐☐

our assemblies ;

☐☐☐ ☐☐☐☐☐☐☐☐☐☐

Transcribe the cursive letters:

and　*this*　*army*　*with*　*a*

⬚⬚⬚　⬚⬚⬚⬚　⬚⬚⬚⬚　⬚⬚⬚⬚　⬚

considerable　*naval*　*armament*

⬚⬚⬚⬚⬚⬚⬚⬚⬚⬚⬚⬚　⬚⬚⬚⬚⬚　⬚⬚⬚⬚⬚⬚⬚⬚

has　*been*　*employed*　*to*　*enforce*

⬚⬚⬚　⬚⬚⬚⬚　⬚⬚⬚⬚⬚⬚⬚⬚　⬚⬚　⬚⬚⬚⬚⬚⬚⬚

the　*collection*　*of*　*taxes* .

⬚⬚⬚　⬚⬚⬚⬚⬚⬚⬚⬚⬚⬚　⬚⬚　⬚⬚⬚⬚⬚

Copy in cursive the above excerpt from the petition to the King.

_____

_____

_____

_____

_____

_____

DECODING CURSIVE LEGEND

Aa	*Bb*	*Cc*	*Dd*	*Ee*	*Ff*	*Gg*	*Hh*	*Ii*	*Jj*	*Kk*	*Ll*	*Mm*
Aa	Bb	Cc	Dd	Ee	Ff	Gg	Hh	Ii	Jj	Kk	Ll	Mm
Nn	*Oo*	*Pp*	*Qq*	*Rr*	*Ss*	*Tt*	*Uu*	*Vv*	*Ww*	*Xx*	*Yy*	*Zz*
Nn	Oo	Pp	Qq	Rr	Ss	Tt	Uu	Vv	Ww	Xx	Yy	Zz

The authority of the commander in chief, and, under him, of the brigadiers general has in time of peace, been rendered supreme in all the civil governments in America.

The commander in chief of all your majestys forces in North.

The authority of the commander and under him,
of the brigadiers general has in time of peace, been rendered
supreme in all the civil governments in America.
The commander in chief of all your majestys forces in
North—

Transcribe the cursive letters:

The   authority   of   the   commander

in   chief   and   under   him,   of   the

brigadiers   general   has   in

time   of   peace,   been   rendered

Transcribe the cursive letters:

supreme   *in*   *all*   *the*   *civil*

governments   *in*   *America .*   *The*

commander   *in*   *chief*   *of*   *all*

your   *majestys*   *forces*   *in*   *North -*

Copy in cursive the above excerpt from the petition to the King.

_____

_____

_____

_____

_____

_____

DECODING CURSIVE LEGEND

Aa	Bb	Cc	Dd	Ee	Ff	Gg	Hh	Ii	Jj	Kk	Ll	Mm
Aa	Bb	Cc	Dd	Ee	Ff	Gg	Hh	Ii	Jj	Kk	Ll	Mm
Nn	Oo	Pp	Qq	Rr	Ss	Tt	Uu	Vv	Ww	Xx	Yy	Zz
Nn	Oo	Pp	Qq	Rr	Ss	Tt	Uu	Vv	Ww	Xx	Yy	Zz

America has, in time of peace been appointed governor of a colony.

The charges of usual offices have been greatly increased; and new expensive and oppressive offices have been multiplied.

America has, in time of peace been appointed governor of a colony. The charges of usual offices have been greatly increased; and new expensive and oppressive offices have been multiplied .

Transcribe the cursive letters.

America   has ,   in   time   of   peace

been   appointed   governor

of   a   colony .   The   charges

of   usual   offices   have

been   greatly   increased;   and

new   expensive   and   oppressive

Transcribe the cursive letters.

offices   *have*   *been*   *multiplied .*

□□□□□□□   □□□□   □□□□   □□□□□□□□□□

Write two cursive copies of the excerpt from the petition to the King, found on pages 70 - 71.

_____

_____

_____

_____

_____

_____

_____

_____

_____

_____

DECODING CURSIVE LEGEND

Aa	*Bb*	*Cc*	*Dd*	*Ee*	*Ff*	*Gg*	*Hh*	*Ii*	*Jj*	*Kk*	*Ll*	*Mm*
Aa	Bb	Cc	Dd	Ee	Ff	Gg	Hh	Ii	Jj	Kk	Ll	Mm
Nn	*Oo*	*Pp*	*Qq*	*Rr*	*Ss*	*Tt*	*Uu*	*Vv*	*Ww*	*Xx*	*Yy*	*Zz*
Nn	Oo	Pp	Qq	Rr	Ss	Tt	Uu	Vv	Ww	Xx	Yy	Zz

The judges of admiralty and vice admiralty courts are im-powered to receive their salaries and fees from the effects condemned by themselves. The officers of the customs are impowered to break open and

The judges of admiralty and vice admiralty courts are im-powered to receive their salaries and fees from the effects condemned by themselves. The offices of the customs are impowered to break open and

Transcribe the cursive letters.

The judges of admiralty and

vice admiralty courts are im-

powered to receive their

salaries and fees from the

effects condemned by

Transcribe the cursive letters.

themselves .

☐☐☐☐☐☐☐☐☐☐

The

☐☐☐

officers

☐☐☐☐☐☐☐☐

of

☐☐

the

☐☐☐

customs

☐☐☐☐☐☐☐

are

☐☐☐

impowered

☐☐☐☐☐☐☐☐☐

to

☐☐

break

☐☐☐☐☐

open

☐☐☐☐

and

☐☐☐

Copy in cursive the excerpt from the petition to the King, found on pages 72 -73.

_____

_____

_____

_____

_____

_____

_____

DECODING CURSIVE LEGEND

Aa	*Bb*	*Cc*	*Dd*	*Ee*	*Ff*	*Gg*	*Hh*	*Ii*	*Jj*	*Kk*	*Ll*	*Mm*
Aa	Bb	Cc	Dd	Ee	Ff	Gg	Hh	Ii	Jj	Kk	Ll	Mm
Nn	*Oo*	*Pp*	*Qq*	*Rr*	*Ss*	*Tt*	*Uu*	*Vv*	*Ww*	*Xx*	*Yy*	*Zz*
Nn	Oo	Pp	Qq	Rr	Ss	Tt	Uu	Vv	Ww	Xx	Yy	Zz

enter houses without the authority of any civil magistrate founded on legal information.

The judges of courts of common law have been made en-tirely dependant on one part of the legislature for their salaries, as well as for the duration of their commissions.

enter houses without the authority of any civil magistrate founded on legal information.

The judges of courts of common law have been made en-tirely dependant on one part of the legislature for the salaries, as well as for the duration of their commissions.

Transcribe the cursive letters in the petition.

enter   houses   without   the

authority   of   any   civil

magistrate   founded   on   legal

information.   The   judges   of

Transcribe the cursive letters.

courts *of* *common* *law* *have*

been *made* *entirely* *dependant*

on *one* *part* *of* *the*

legislature *for* *the* *salaries* ,

as *well* *as* *for* *the* *duration*

of *their* *commissions* .

In this excerpt, find a word, spelled differently than the way we spell it today.
Find the hyphenated word and write it as it not hyphenated.

_____

_____

DECODING CURSIVE LEGEND

Aa	*Bb*	*Cc*	*Dd*	*Ee*	*Ff*	*Gg*	*Hh*	*Ii*	*Jj*	*Kk*	*Ll*	*Mm*
Aa	Bb	Cc	Dd	Ee	Ff	Gg	Hh	Ii	Jj	Kk	Ll	Mm
Nn	*Oo*	*Pp*	*Qq*	*Rr*	*Ss*	*Tt*	*Uu*	*Vv*	*Ww*	*Xx*	*Yy*	*Zz*
Nn	Oo	Pp	Qq	Rr	Ss	Tt	Uu	Vv	Ww	Xx	Yy	Zz

To the Kings most excellent majesty

Most gracious Sovereign

We your majestys faithful subjects of the colonies of New-hampshire, Massachusetts-bay, Rhode-island and providence plantations, Connecticut, New-York, New-Jersey, Pennsylvania, the counties of New-Castle, Kent and Sussex on Delaware, Maryland, Virginia, North-Carolina and South-Carolina in behalf of ourselves and the inhabitants of those colonies who have deputed us to represent them in General Congress, by this our humble petition, beg leave to lay our grievances before the throne.

A standing army has been kept in these colonies, ever since the conclusion of the late war, without the consent of our assemblies; and this army with a considerable naval armament has been employed to enforce the collection of taxes.

The authority of the commander in chief, and, under him, of the brigadiers general has in time of peace, been rendered supreme in all the civil governments in America.

The commander in chief of all your majestys forces in North America has, in time of peace been appointed governor of a colony.

The charges of usual offices have been greatly increased; and new, expensive and oppressive offices have been multiplied.

The judges of admiralty and vice admiralty courts are impowered to receive their salaries and fees from the effects condemned by themselves. The officers of the customs are impowered to break open and enter houses without the authority of any civil Magistrate founded on legal information.

The judges of courts of common law have been made entirely dependant on one part of the legislature for their salaries, as well as for the duration of their commissions.

Read the first page of the Petition to the King, paying attention to spelling and grammar discrepancies that today would be considered errors. If you are having a hard time reading this old document, you might need to use a magnifying glass to help you see better Write a cursive copy of the text by today's standards of proper English.

_____

_____

_____

_____

_____

_____

_____

_____

_____

_____

_____

_____

_____

_____

_____

_____

_____

Imagine you are the King of England at the end of 18th century. How would you feel to receive such letter from America? In your best cursive, write a letter to respond to the Colonies' petition with decisions you would've made if you were in charge.

_____

_____

_____

_____

_____

_____

_____

_____

_____

_____

_____

_____

_____

_____

_____

_____

_____

Primary Source

2.

George Washington's Farewell Address
September 19, 1796

GEORGE WASHINGTON'S FAREWELL ADDRESS, SEPTEMBER 19, 1796

American presidents serve no more than two consecutive terms because of the example set by our first president from the beginning. In 1796, as his second term was coming to an end, he refused to run for a third time. George Washington was a very popular president, and many people encouraged him, even pleaded with him, to stay in office for another term. However, Washington knew that if he was to grow old and die while serving in the White House, people might see the presidency as a lifelong appointment, not very different from a monarchy. Therefore, the president reasoned, American citizens needed to see a clear difference between the old ways of European tyrannies and their new republic. He wanted to make sure that the people could witness a democratic, peaceful transfer of power. This is why Washington's Farewell Address is regarded today as a historic gesture reinforcing that we are a constitutional republic and not a monarchy by another name. Nor is it a pure democracy, led by mob rule, as with the tragic failure of the French Revolution. Following this logic, it is reasonable to ask if other career politicians (like lifelong senators and representatives) might also reminisce of a permanent ruling class, very similar to the European aristocracies.

In this book, we'll study page 13 of Washington's Farewell Address. In it, when you read the words of Washington, pay attention to the warning of the danger of one branch of the government going against the Constitution and usurping the power of the other branches. We chose this page because today, the alarm George Washington sounded more than two centuries ago is as urgent and relevant as ever.

For example, when you hear a president announcing that he doesn't need Congress to make law and that he has "a phone and a pen", this is a person who openly declares that he wants to rule with a presidential decree, like a king. Effectively, he is taking over the role of Congress in making laws. This is a grasp for power that Washington was referring to.

Another example is when you hear a president or a supportive congressperson promoting the "packing of the Supreme court". Filling the court with people who will "rubber stamp" your decisions is equal to absorbing the powers of the judicial branch to add them to your own. This would be another instance of the tyranny that Washington warned us about.

So what can be done about it?

Notice that Washington wasn't warning future presidents following after him so much as he was warning us -the People of the United States- to be on guard, ready to recognize when the illegitimate consolidation of power is being attempted by one branch of the government. He was warning those who followed after him to be vigilant and guard our republic against despots.

Page 13 from George Washington's farewell address, September 17, 1796.

...

It is important, likewise, that the habits of thinking in a free country should inspire caution in those entrusted with its administration, to confine themselves within their respective constitutional spheres.

Transcribe the selected cursive excerpt from Washington's Farewell address:

It is important, likewise, that

☐☐ ☐☐ ☐☐☐☐☐☐☐☐☐ ☐☐☐☐☐☐☐☐ ☐☐☐☐

the habits of thinking in a

☐☐☐ ☐☐☐☐☐☐ ☐☐ ☐☐☐☐☐☐☐☐ ☐☐ ☐

free country should inspire

☐☐☐☐ ☐☐☐☐☐☐☐ ☐☐☐☐☐☐ ☐☐☐☐☐☐☐

caution in those entrusted

☐☐☐☐☐☐☐ ☐☐ ☐☐☐☐☐ ☐☐☐☐☐☐☐☐☐

Transcribe the cursive letters.

with   its   administration,   to

☐☐☐☐ ☐☐☐ ☐☐☐☐☐☐☐☐☐☐☐☐☐☐ ☐☐

confine   themselves   within

☐☐☐☐☐☐☐ ☐☐☐☐☐☐☐☐☐☐ ☐☐☐☐☐☐

their   respective

☐☐☐☐☐ ☐☐☐☐☐☐☐☐☐☐

constitutional   spheres,

☐☐☐☐☐☐☐☐☐☐☐☐☐☐ ☐☐☐☐☐☐☐

Copy in cursive the above excerpt from Washington's farewell address.

_____

_____

_____

_____

_____

_____

DECODING CURSIVE LEGEND

Aa	*Bb*	*Cc*	*Dd*	*Ee*	*Ff*	*Gg*	*Hh*	*Ii*	*Jj*	*Kk*	*Ll*	*Mm*
Aa	Bb	Cc	Dd	Ee	Ff	Gg	Hh	Ii	Jj	Kk	Ll	Mm
Nn	*Oo*	*Pp*	*Qq*	*Rr*	*Ss*	*Tt*	*Uu*	*Vv*	*Ww*	*Xx*	*Yy*	*Zz*
Nn	Oo	Pp	Qq	Rr	Ss	Tt	Uu	Vv	Ww	Xx	Yy	Zz

avoiding in the exercise of the powers of one department

to encroach upon another. The spirit of encroachment

tends to consolidate the powers of all the departments in

one and thus to create, whatever the form of govern-

(ment)

Transcribe the above cursive excerpt from Washington's Farewell address:

avoiding *in* *the* *exercise* *of*

the *powers* *of* *one* *department*

to *encroach* *upon* *another.* *The*

spirit *of* *encroachment* *tends*

Transcribe the cursive letters.

to   *consolidate*   *the*   *powers*   *of*

all   *the*   *departments*   *in*   *one*

and   *thus*   *to*   *create,*   *whatever*

the   *form*   *of*   *govern - (ment)*

Copy in cursive the above excerpt from Washington's farewell address.

DECODING CURSIVE LEGEND

Aa	Bb	Cc	Dd	Ee	Ff	Gg	Hh	Ii	Jj	Kk	Ll	Mm
Aa	Bb	Cc	Dd	Ee	Ff	Gg	Hh	Ii	Jj	Kk	Ll	Mm
Nn	Oo	Pp	Qq	Rr	Ss	Tt	Uu	Vv	Ww	Xx	Yy	Zz
Nn	Oo	Pp	Qq	Rr	Ss	Tt	Uu	Vv	Ww	Xx	Yy	Zz

ment, a real despotism. A just estimate of that love of power, and proneness to abuse it, which predominates in the human heart, is sufficient to satisfy us of the truth of this position. The necessity of reciprocal checks in the

(govern -) ment, a real despotism. A just estimate of that

love of power and proneness to abuse it which predominates

in the human heart is sufficient to satisfy us of the truth of

this position. The necessity of reciprocal checks in the

Transcribe the above cursive excerpt from Washington's Farewell address:

(govern -) ment,   a   real   despotism.

A   just   estimate   of   that   love

of   power   and   proneness   to

abuse   it   which   predominates

in   the   human   heart   is

Transcribe the cursive letters.

sufficient   *to*   *satisfy*   *us*

of   *the*   *truth*   *of*   *this*

position.   *The*   *necessity*   *of*

reciprocal   *checks*   *in*   *the*

Copy in cursive the above excerpt from Washington's farewell address.

_____

_____

_____

_____

_____

_____

DECODING CURSIVE LEGEND

Aa	Bb	Cc	Dd	Ee	Ff	Gg	Hh	Ii	Jj	Kk	Ll	Mm
Aa	Bb	Cc	Dd	Ee	Ff	Gg	Hh	Ii	Jj	Kk	Ll	Mm
Nn	Oo	Pp	Qq	Rr	Ss	Tt	Uu	Vv	Ww	Xx	Yy	Zz
Nn	Oo	Pp	Qq	Rr	Ss	Tt	Uu	Vv	Ww	Xx	Yy	Zz

exercise of political power; by dividing and distributing it into different depositories, and constituting each the guardian of the public weal against invasions by the others, has been evinced by experiments ancient and modern: some

exercise of political power; by dividing and distributing

it into different depositories and constituting each the

guardian of the public weal against invasions by the others

has been evinced by experiments ancient and modern, some

Transcribe the above cursive excerpt from Washington's Farewell address:

exercise   of   political   power;

by   dividing   and   distributing

it   into   different

depositories   and

constituting   each

Transcribe the cursive letters.

the *guardian* *of* *the* *public*

weal *against* *invasions* *by*

the *others,* *has* *been* *evinced*

by *experiments* *ancient* *and*

modern, *some*

Copy in cursive the above excerpt from Washington's farewell address.

_____

_____

_____

_____

_____

DECODING CURSIVE LEGEND

Aa	Bb	Cc	Dd	Ee	Ff	Gg	Hh	Ii	Jj	Kk	Ll	Mm
Aa	Bb	Cc	Dd	Ee	Ff	Gg	Hh	Ii	Jj	Kk	Ll	Mm
Nn	Oo	Pp	Qq	Rr	Ss	Tt	Uu	Vv	Ww	Xx	Yy	Zz
Nn	Oo	Pp	Qq	Rr	Ss	Tt	Uu	Vv	Ww	Xx	Yy	Zz

of them in our country and under our own eyes. To preserve them must be as necessary as to institute them. If, in the opinion of the People, the distribution or modification of the constitutional powers be in any particular

some of them in our country and under our own eyes. To

preserve them must be as necessary as to institute them. If

in the opinion of the people the distribution or modification

of the constitutional powers be in any particular

Transcribe the above cursive excerpt from Washington's Farewell address:

some   of   them   in   our   country   and

under   our   own   eyes.   To   preserve

them   must   be   as   necessary   as

to   institute   them.   If   in   the

Transcribe the cursive letters.

opinion   *of*   *the*   *people*   *the*

distribution   *or*

modification   *of*   *the*

constitutional   *powers*

be   *in*   *any*   *particular*

Copy in cursive the above excerpt from Washington's farewell address.

_____

_____

_____

_____

_____

DECODING CURSIVE LEGEND

Aa	Bb	Cc	Dd	Ee	Ff	Gg	Hh	Ii	Jj	Kk	Ll	Mm
Aa	Bb	Cc	Dd	Ee	Ff	Gg	Hh	Ii	Jj	Kk	Ll	Mm
Nn	Oo	Pp	Qq	Rr	Ss	Tt	Uu	Vv	Ww	Xx	Yy	Zz
Nn	Oo	Pp	Qq	Rr	Ss	Tt	Uu	Vv	Ww	Xx	Yy	Zz

*wrong, let it be corrected by an amendment in the way
which the Constitution designates. But let there be no
change by usurpation; for though this, in one instance,
may be the instrument of good, it is the customary*

Transcribe the above cursive excerpt from Washington's Farewell address:

wrong, let *it* *be* *corrected* *by*

an *amendment* *in* *the* *way* *which*

the *Constitution* *designates.*

But *let* *there* *be* *no* *change* *by*

Transcribe the cursive letters.

usurpation; *for* *though* *this,*

in *one* *instance,* *may* *be* *the*

instrument *of* *good,* *it* *is*

the *customary*

Copy in cursive the above excerpt from Washington's farewell address.

DECODING CURSIVE LEGEND

Aa	*Bb*	*Cc*	*Dd*	*Ee*	*Ff*	*Gg*	*Hh*	*Ii*	*Jj*	*Kk*	*Ll*	*Mm*
A a	B b	C c	D d	E e	F f	G g	H h	I i	J j	K k	L l	M m
Nn	*Oo*	*Pp*	*Qq*	*Rr*	*Ss*	*Tt*	*Uu*	*Vv*	*Ww*	*Xx*	*Yy*	*Zz*
N n	O o	P p	Q q	R r	S s	T t	U u	V v	W w	X x	Y y	Z z

weapon by which free governments are destroyed. The precedent must always greatly overbalance in permanent evil any partial or transient benefit which the use can at any time yield.

Transcribe the above cursive excerpt from Washington's Farewell address:

weapon   by   which   free

governments   are   destroyed.

The   precedent   must   always

greatly   overbalance   in

permanent   evil   any   partial

Transcribe the cursive letters.

or   transient   benefit   which

☐☐ ☐☐☐☐☐☐☐☐☐   ☐☐☐☐☐☐☐   ☐☐☐☐☐

the   use   can   at   any   time   yield.

☐☐☐ ☐☐☐ ☐☐☐ ☐☐ ☐☐☐ ☐☐☐☐ ☐☐☐☐☐

Copy in cursive the above excerpt from Washington's farewell address.

_____

_____

_____

_____

_____

_____

_____

DECODING CURSIVE LEGEND

Aa	*Bb*	*Cc*	*Dd*	*Ee*	*Ff*	*Gg*	*Hh*	*Ii*	*Jj*	*Kk*	*Ll*	*Mm*
Aa	Bb	Cc	Dd	Ee	Ff	Gg	Hh	Ii	Jj	Kk	Ll	Mm
Nn	*Oo*	*Pp*	*Qq*	*Rr*	*Ss*	*Tt*	*Uu*	*Vv*	*Ww*	*Xx*	*Yy*	*Zz*
Nn	Oo	Pp	Qq	Rr	Ss	Tt	Uu	Vv	Ww	Xx	Yy	Zz

Of all the dispositions and habits which lead to political prosperity, Religion and Morality are indispensable supports. — In vain would that Man

Of all the dispositions and habits which lead to political prosperity, religion and morality are indispensable supports. In vain would that man …

Transcribe the above cursive excerpt from Washington's Farewell address:

Of all the dispositions

and habits which lead to

political prosperity,

religion and morality are

indispensable supports.

Transcribe the cursive letters.

In   vain   would   that   man ...

☐☐ ☐☐☐☐ ☐☐☐☐☐ ☐☐☐☐ ☐☐☐

For your information, on the next page of the original document, the sentence finishes with:

... claim the tribute of Patriotism , who should labour to subvert these great Pillars of human happiness, these firmest props of the duties of Men & citizens.

Copy in cursive the above excerpt from Washington's farewell address.

_____

_____

_____

_____

_____

_____

DECODING CURSIVE LEGEND

Aa	*Bb*	*Cc*	*Dd*	*Ee*	*Ff*	*Gg*	*Hh*	*Ii*	*Jj*	*Kk*	*Ll*	*Mm*
Aa	Bb	Cc	Dd	Ee	Ff	Gg	Hh	Ii	Jj	Kk	Ll	Mm
Nn	*Oo*	*Pp*	*Qq*	*Rr*	*Ss*	*Tt*	*Uu*	*Vv*	*Ww*	*Xx*	*Yy*	*Zz*
Nn	Oo	Pp	Qq	Rr	Ss	Tt	Uu	Vv	Ww	Xx	Yy	Zz

It is important likewise, that the habits of thinking in a free country, should inspire caution in those entrusted with its administration, to confine themselves within their respective constitutional spheres, avoiding in the exercise of the powers of one department to encroach upon another. The spirit of encroachment tends to consolidate the powers of all the departments in one, and thus to create, whatever the form of Government, a real despotism. A just estimate of that love of power, and proneness to abuse it, which predominates in the human heart, is sufficient to satisfy us of the truth of this position. The necessity of reciprocal checks in the exercise of political power; by dividing and distributing it into different depositories, and constituting each the guardian of the public weal against invasions by the others, has been evinced by experiments ancient and modern; some of them in our country and under our own eyes. To preserve them must be as necessary as to institute them. If, in the opinion of the People, the distribution or modification of the constitutional powers be in any particular wrong, let it be corrected by an amendment in the way which the constitution designates.— But let there be no change by usurpation; for though this, in one instance, may be the instrument of good, it is the customary weapon by which free governments are destroyed.— The precedent must always greatly overbalance in permanent evil any partial or transient benefit which the use can at any time yield.—

Of all the dispositions and habits which lead to political prosperity, Religion and Morality are indispensable supports.— In vain would that

Man

Can you read the 13th page from the draft of Washington's farewell address without help? Try copying the text in cursive.

Imagine that you are living during the end of George Washington's administration. Write him a send-off note in cursive, with your gratitude, well-wishes for his future and asking him any questions you might have for him.

_____

_____

_____

_____

_____

_____

_____

_____

_____

_____

_____

_____

_____

_____

_____

_____

Primary Source

3.

Thomas Jefferson's Letter
to the Danbury Baptist Association
January 1, 1802

Jefferson's Letter to the Danbury Baptists

The primary documents left to us by the Founding Fathers date well over 200 years ago. Centuries-old papers usually aren't in their pristine condition, and sometimes it could be very difficult to read them. Today's condition of our primary sources depends on the quality of the paper, composition of the ink, humidity, temperature, sunlight, and other environmental conditions of the storage where they were kept. In such cases, historians and archivists resort to using imaging devices like X-rays, electron microscopes and scanners, chemical treatments of the paper and other techniques to improve the readability of old documents. The next document we'll examine is in such poor condition. However, we chose to include it in this book because it is one of the most important primary sources to see with our own eyes and to understand because it's one of the most misquoted, misunderstood and misconstrued texts amongst the Founding Fathers' works. I'm talking about the "wall of separation between church and state". In October of 1801, leaders from the Danbury Baptist Association had written to Thomas Jefferson, expressing their concerns about the attitude of the Connecticut establishment towards anyone who wasn't going to the Congregationalist church. In response, he wrote back a letter reassuring them of their First Amendment right to freely exercise their religion and their Government's inability to prohibit them from doing so. Thomas Jefferson's letter to the Danbury Baptists is not very easy to read. Still, it's so very important to our understanding of history that we should give it a go.

 Ironically, this letter is the most quoted document as "proof" that our Founding Fathers wanted religion to play no role in governing our country. Many, who love to quote it, claim it to be taken directly from the American Constitution. It is important to point out that this is a private letter, revealing Jefferson's heart, not a legal clause in any of the founding documents.

Nevertheless, reading the actual words of Jefferson in the context of his own thoughts clearly expresses the exact opposite idea from the one popularly pushed today. It is common today to hear teachers and politicians preach that the "separation of church and state" goes both ways. Religious beliefs, they'd say, are not permitted to influence political decisions in this country. Actually, only the government has no role in establishing and regulating religion. Only the government is constitutionally prevented from interfering in the Baptists' free expression of worship. The first amendment to the Constitution does not prevent the religious beliefs of American citizens from guiding their political choices. The "wall of separation" is meant to keep

politicians' hands out of our churches, not religion, out of the politician's consciousness. Jefferson believed faith to be a private matter between a man and his God. If a public servant's beliefs required him

to vote in a certain way - that was his God-given, inalienable right. The same applies regardless if this person happened to serve as a President, a judge, or a representative in Congress. In such cases, the Constitution guarantees their right to vote their consciousness while on the job. Suppose a community wishes to raise a cross in the middle of a veterans' cemetery; or to display the Ten Commandments in the lobby of their courthouse: It is the right of the people in this community to do so. Their exercise of religion cannot be prohibited by the Government.

We have a better copy of the first rough draft of Jefferson's letter, but it is very difficult to work through all the scratches and handwritten edits. The cleaner draft of the letter is in worse physical condition, but by using both copies, like real historians, we'll do our best and try to piece things together and decipher it. If the text in the image is too smudged to read, you can reference the rough draft. If that doesn't work either, just use the cursive transcription of the passage you are working on. Let's read and decide for ourselves the truth about Jefferson's opinion on church and state!

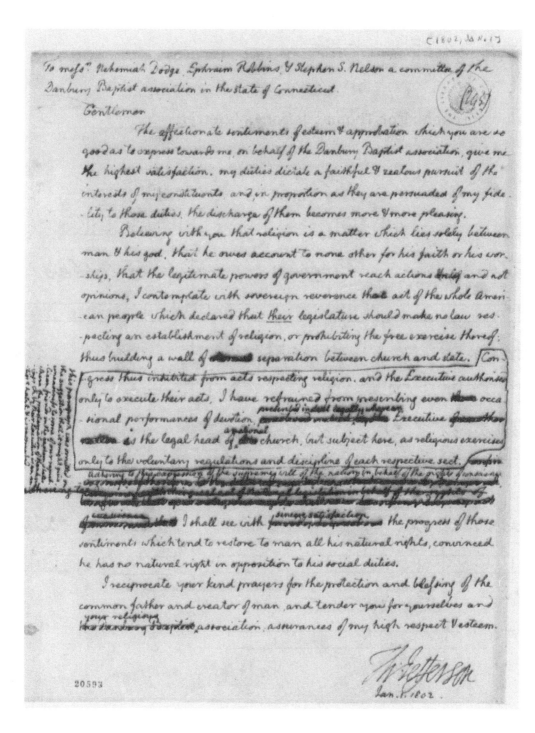

To mess.ʳˢ Nehemiah Dodge, Ephraim Robbins, & Stephen S. Nelson a committee of the Danbury Baptist association in the state of Connecticut.

To Mess. Nehemiah Dodge, Ephraim Robbins, & Stephen S. Nelson, a committee of the Danbury Baptist association in the state of Connecticut.

Transcribe the opening of Thomas Jefferson's letter:

To Mess. Nehemiah Dodge,

Ephraim Robbins, & Stephen S.

Nelson, a committee of the

Danbury Baptist

association in the state

of Connecticut.

Copy in cursive the opening of Thomas Jefferson's letter.

_____

_____

_____

_____

_____

Read and copy your cursive text above.

_____

_____

_____

_____

_____

DECODING CURSIVE LEGEND

Aa	*Bb*	*Cc*	*Dd*	*Ee*	*Ff*	*Gg*	*Hh*	*Ii*	*Jj*	*Kk*	*Ll*	*Mm*
A a	B b	C c	D d	E e	F f	G g	H h	I i	J j	K k	L l	M m
Nn	*Oo*	*Pp*	*Qq*	*Rr*	*Ss*	*Tt*	*Uu*	*Vv*	*Ww*	*Xx*	*Yy*	*Zz*
N n	O o	P p	Q q	R r	S s	T t	U u	V v	W w	X x	Y y	Z z

Gentlemen

The affectionate sentiments of esteem & approbation which you are so good as to express towards me, on behalf of the Danbury Baptist association, give me the highest satisfaction. my duties dictate a faithful & zealous pursuit of the

Gentlemen

The affectionate sentiments of esteem & approbation which you are so good as to express towards me, on behalf of the Danbury Baptist association, give me the highest satisfaction. My duties dictate a faithful and zealous pursuit of the

Transcribe the above opening address of Thomas Jefferson's letter.

Gentlemen

The   affectionate   sentiments

of   esteem   and   approbation

which   you   are   so   good   as   to

Transcribe the opening of Thomas Jefferson's letter:

express   towards   me, on   behalf

of   the   Danbury   Baptist

association.   give   me   the

highest   satisfaction.   My

duties   dictate   a   faithful

and   zealous   pursuit   of   the

Who is Thomas Jefferson's letter addressed to ?

_____

DECODING CURSIVE LEGEND

A a	B b	C c	D d	E e	F f	G g	H h	I i	J j	K k	L l	M m
A a	B b	C c	D d	E e	F f	G g	H h	I i	J j	K k	L l	M m
N n	O o	P p	Q q	R r	S s	T t	U u	V v	W w	X x	Y y	Z z
N n	O o	P p	Q q	R r	S s	T t	U u	V v	W w	X x	Y y	Z z

interests of my constituents, and in proportion as they are persuaded of my fide-lity to those duties. the discharge of them becomes more & more pleasing.

Believing with you that religion is a matter which lies solely between

interests of my constituents . and in proportion as they are

persuaded of my fide-

lity to those duties . the discharge of them becomes more and more

pleasing . Believing with you that religion is a matter which lies

solely between

Transcribe the above excerpt of Thomas Jefferson's letter.

interests   of   my   constituents .

and   in   proportion   as   they

are   persuaded   of   my   fidelity

to   pleasing.   Believing   with

you *that* *religion* *is* *a*

☐☐☐   ☐☐☐☐   ☐☐☐☐☐☐☐☐   ☐☐   ☐

matter *which* *lies* *solely*

☐☐☐☐☐☐   ☐☐☐☐☐   ☐☐☐☐   ☐☐☐☐☐☐

between

☐☐☐☐☐☐☐

Copy in cursive the excerpt from Jefferson's letter, found on pages 108 - 109.

_____

_____

_____

_____

_____

_____

_____

DECODING CURSIVE LEGEND

Aa	*Bb*	*Cc*	*Dd*	*Ee*	*Ff*	*Gg*	*Hh*	*Ii*	*Jj*	*Kk*	*Ll*	*Mm*
Aa	Bb	Cc	Dd	Ee	Ff	Gg	Hh	Ii	Jj	Kk	Ll	Mm
Nn	*Oo*	*Pp*	*Qq*	*Rr*	*Ss*	*Tt*	*Uu*	*Vv*	*Ww*	*Xx*	*Yy*	*Zz*
Nn	Oo	Pp	Qq	Rr	Ss	Tt	Uu	Vv	Ww	Xx	Yy	Zz

man & his god, that he owes account to none other for his faith or his wor-

-ship, that the legitimate powers of government reach actions <del>truly</del> and not opinions, I contemplate with sovereign reverence that act of the whole Ameri-

man & his God. that he owes account to none other for his

faith or his wor-

ship. that the legitimate powers of government reach actions

only and not opinions. I contemplate with sovereign reverence

that act of the whole Ameri- (-can)

Transcribe the above section of Thomas Jefferson's letter.

& his God. that he owes account

to none other for his faith

or his worship. that the

legitimate powers of

government reach actions

Continue to transcribe this excerpt of Thomas Jefferson's letter:

only □□□□□ *and* □□□ *not* □□□ *opinions.* □□□□□□□□□ *I* □

contemplate □□□□□□□□□□ *with* □□□□ *sovereign* □□□□□□□□□

reverence □□□□□□□□□ *that* □□□□ *act* □□□ *of* □□ *the* □□□

whole □□□□□ *American* □□□□□□□□

Copy in cursive the excerpt from Thomas Jefferson's letter.

_____

_____

_____

_____

_____

_____

DECODING CURSIVE LEGEND

Aa	*Bb*	*Cc*	*Dd*	*Ee*	*Ff*	*Gg*	*Hh*	*Ii*	*Jj*	*Kk*	*Ll*	*Mm*
Aa	Bb	Cc	Dd	Ee	Ff	Gg	Hh	Ii	Jj	Kk	Ll	Mm
Nn	*Oo*	*Pp*	*Qq*	*Rr*	*Ss*	*Tt*	*Uu*	*Vv*	*Ww*	*Xx*	*Yy*	*Zz*
Nn	Oo	Pp	Qq	Rr	Ss	Tt	Uu	Vv	Ww	Xx	Yy	Zz

can people which declared that their legislature should make no law res-
-pecting an establishment of religion, or prohibiting the free exercise thereof,
thus building a wall of ~~separation~~ separation between church and state. [Con-]

(Ameri-)

-can people which declared that their legislature should make no law res-

-pecting an establishment of religion, or prohibiting the free exercise thereof, thus building a wall of ████████ separation between church and state.

Transcribe the above excerpt of Thomas Jefferson's letter.

which *declared* *that* *their*

legislature *should"* *make* *no*

law *respecting* *an*

establishment *of* *religion,* *or*

prohibiting *the* *free*

Continue to transcribe the above section of Thomas Jefferson's letter.

exercise

thereof,

" thus

building   *a*   *wall*   *of*   *separation*

between   *church*   *and*   *state.*

Copy in cursive the above excerpt of Thomas Jefferson's letter.

_____

_____

_____

_____

_____

_____

_____

DECODING CURSIVE LEGEND

Aa	*Bb*	*Cc*	*Dd*	*Ee*	*Ff*	*Gg*	*Hh*	*Ii*	*Jj*	*Kk*	*Ll*	*Mm*
Aa	Bb	Cc	Dd	Ee	Ff	Gg	Hh	Ii	Jj	Kk	Ll	Mm

Nn	*Oo*	*Pp*	*Qq*	*Rr*	*Ss*	*Tt*	*Uu*	*Vv*	*Ww*	*Xx*	*Yy*	*Zz*
Nn	Oo	Pp	Qq	Rr	Ss	Tt	Uu	Vv	Ww	Xx	Yy	Zz

This sentence, apparently, was finalized only after some serious thinking and rethinking. In the first draft we find an extra passage that was removed from the final letter. The original paragraph was replaced with a single sentence found in the rough draft, crammed between a few edited lines. Compare the two images and see which one is easier to read. You might need to use a magnifying glass for this one!

adhering to this expression of the supreme will of the nation in behalf of the rights of conscience.

Transcribe the above excerpt of Thomas Jefferson's letter:

adhering to this expression of the supreme will of the nation in behalf of the rights of conscience.

I shall see with sincere satisfaction the progress of those sentiments which tend to restore to man all his natural rights, convinced he has no natural right in opposition to his social duties.

I shall see with sincere satisfaction the progress of those

sentiments which tend to restore to man all his natural rights,

convinced he has no natural right in opposition to his social duties.

Transcribe the above excerpt of Thomas Jefferson's letter:

I shall see with sincere

satisfaction the progress of

those sentiments which tend

to restore to man all his

natural rights, convinced he

has no natural right in

Transcribe the above excerpt of Thomas Jefferson's letter:

opposition

☐☐☐☐☐☐☐☐☐☐

to ☐☐

his ☐☐☐

social ☐☐☐☐☐☐

duties

☐☐☐☐☐☐

Copy in cursive the excerpt of Thomas Jefferson's letter. Refer to pages 116-118.

_____

_____

_____

_____

_____

_____

_____

_____

DECODING CURSIVE LEGEND

Aa	*Bb*	*Cc*	*Dd*	*Ee*	*Ff*	*Gg*	*Hh*	*Ii*	*Jj*	*Kk*	*Ll*	*Mm*
Aa	Bb	Cc	Dd	Ee	Ff	Gg	Hh	Ii	Jj	Kk	Ll	Mm
Nn	*Oo*	*Pp*	*Qq*	*Rr*	*Ss*	*Tt*	*Uu*	*Vv*	*Ww*	*Xx*	*Yy*	*Zz*
Nn	Oo	Pp	Qq	Rr	Ss	Tt	Uu	Vv	Ww	Xx	Yy	Zz

I reciprocate your kind prayers for the protection and blessing of the common father and creator of man, and tender you for yourselves and your religious association, assurances of my high respect Vesteem.

Th.Jefferson

Jan. 1. 1802.

20593

I reciprocate your kind prayers for the protection and

blessing of the common father and creator of man, and

tender you for yourselves and your religious association,

assurances of my high respect & esteem.

Th.Jefferson

Jan. 1. 1802.

Transcribe the above section of Thomas Jefferson's letter:

I reciprocate your kind

prayers for the protection

and blessing of the common

Transcribe the excerpt of Thomas Jefferson's letter.

father　*and*　*creator*　*of*　*man.*　*and*

tender　*you*　*for*　*yourselves*

and　*your*　*religious*

association.　*assurances*　*of*

my　*high*　*respect*　*&*　*esteem.*

Th.　*Jefferson*　*Jan.*　*1.*　*1802.*

Copy the ending of Thomas Jefferson's letter from pages 119-120.

_____

_____

_____

_____

_____

Read the transcript of Jefferson's letter to the Danbury Baptist Association. Pay attention to spelling and grammar discrepancies which today would be considered errors.

To messers. Nehemiah Dodge. Ephraim Robbins. & Stephen S. Nelson. a committee of the Danbury Baptist association in the state of Connecticut.

Gentlemen

The affectionate sentiments of esteem and approbation which you are so good as to express towards me. on behalf of the Danbury Baptist association. give me the highest satisfaction. my duties dictate a faithful and zealous pursuit of the interests of my constituents. & in proportion as they are persuaded of my fidelity to those duties. the discharge of them becomes more and more pleasing.

Believing with you that religion is a matter which lies solely between Man & his God. that he owes account to none other for his faith or his worship. that the legitimate powers of government reach actions only. & not opinions. I contemplate with sovereign reverence that act of the whole American people which declared that their legislature should "make no law respecting an establishment of religion. or prohibiting the free exercise thereof." thus building a wall of separation between Church & State. Adhering to this expression of the supreme will of the nation in behalf of the rights of conscience. I shall see with sincere satisfaction the progress of those sentiments which tend to restore to man all his natural rights. convinced he has no natural right in opposition to his social duties.

I reciprocate your kind prayers for the protection & blessing of the common father and creator of man. and tender you for yourselves & your religious association. assurances of my high respect & esteem.

Th. Jefferson
Jan. 1. 1802.

In cursive, write a letter to Jefferson. Ask any questions or objections you might have about his stands on religion and state.

Primary Source

4.

Frederick Douglass' Letter
to his former owner Hugh Auld
October 4, 1857

FREDERICK DOUGLASS LETTER TO HIS FORMER OWNER, OCTOBER 4, 1857

Frederick Douglass is often referred to as one of our black Founding Fathers. He escaped slavery in 1837 and moved to New York, where he raised money to purchase his freedom from Hugh Auld.

Twenty years later, Mr. Douglass wrote a letter to his former master, where this great man's profound wisdom and humanity were revealed for us to discover. In this letter, he expresses his love and respect for the Auld family. Now a free man, he asks questions about the children and wife of his former master. Reading his words, we can feel how he regrets losing his connection with them and how he misses them.

Finally, we witness his personal testimony regarding his feelings about slavery and freedom. Reading about slavery in textbooks, watching movies and listening to other historians' interpretations is fine. However, there is no better way to be transported into the past, to feel and understand the evils of slavery and the precious value of freedom than studying primary sources like this letter. From just one page filled with the thoughts of a formerly enslaved man, there is so much more to learn! Frederick Douglass had beautiful, easy-to-read penmanship, so this letter will be much easier to follow than Jefferson's :)

Finally, we witness his personal testimony regarding his feelings about slavery and freedom.

What is most significant about Douglass is his spirit of love and forgiveness. Frederick Douglass shows himself to be a man who can rise above circumstance and do it with a heart of greatness. He does not present himself as a victim with a heart full of bitterness and hate. How different from the masses of people today that justify crimes against others of all colors, including their own, while proclaiming their victimhood.

Here is a man that the modern age can learn from and would do well to emulate.

Rochester Oct. 4th (1857

Hugh Auld Esq
My dear sir.
My heart tells me that you are too noble to treat with indifference the request I am about to make, It is twenty years

Rochester Oct. 4th (1857

Hugh Auld Esq ,
My dear Sir.
my heart tells me that you are too noble to treat with indifference the request I am about to make , it is twenty years

Transcribe the opening of Frederick Douglas' letter.

Rochester   Oct.   4   th   1857

Hugh   Auld   Esq,   My   dear   Sir.

My   heart   tells   me   that   you

Transcribe the cursive letters:

are   *too*   *noble*   *to*   *treat*   *with*

indifference   *the*   *request*   *I*

am   *about*   *to*   *make,*   *it*   *is*

twenty   *years*

Copy in cursive the opening from Frederick Douglass' letter.

_____

_____

_____

_____

_____

_____

_____

DECODING CURSIVE LEGEND

Aa	*Bb*	*Cc*	*Dd*	*Ee*	*Ff*	*Gg*	*Hh*	*Ii*	*Jj*	*Kk*	*Ll*	*Mm*
Aa	Bb	Cc	Dd	Ee	Ff	Gg	Hh	Ii	Jj	Kk	Ll	Mm
Nn	*Oo*	*Pp*	*Qq*	*Rr*	*Ss*	*Tt*	*Uu*	*Vv*	*Ww*	*Xx*	*Yy*	*Zz*
Nn	Oo	Pp	Qq	Rr	Ss	Tt	Uu	Vv	Ww	Xx	Yy	Zz

Since I ranaway from you, or rather not from you but from Slavery, and since then I have often felt a strong desire to hold a little correspondence with you and to learn something of the position and prospects

since I ranaway from you , or rather not from you but from slavery , and since then I have often felt a strong desire to hold a little correspondence with you and to learn something of the position and prospects

Transcribe the excerpt from Frederick Douglas' letter.

since   I   ranaway   from   you   or

rather   not   from   you   but   from

slavery,   and   since   then   I   have

often   felt   a   strong   desire   to

hold   a   little   correspondence

with   you   and   to   learn

Transcribe the cursive letters.

something

☐☐☐☐☐☐☐☐☐

of

☐☐

the

☐☐☐

position

☐☐☐☐☐☐☐☐

and

☐☐☐

prospects

☐☐☐☐☐☐☐☐☐

Copy in cursive the above excerpt from Frederick Douglass' letter.

_____

_____

_____

_____

_____

_____

_____

DECODING CURSIVE LEGEND

Aa	*Bb*	*Cc*	*Dd*	*Ee*	*Ff*	*Gg*	*Hh*	*Ii*	*Jj*	*Kk*	*Ll*	*Mm*
Aa	Bb	Cc	Dd	Ee	Ff	Gg	Hh	Ii	Jj	Kk	Ll	Mm
Nn	*Oo*	*Pp*	*Qq*	*Rr*	*Ss*	*Tt*	*Uu*	*Vv*	*Ww*	*Xx*	*Yy*	*Zz*
Nn	Oo	Pp	Qq	Rr	Ss	Tt	Uu	Vv	Ww	Xx	Yy	Zz

of your dear children . They were dear to me – and are still – indeed I
feel nothing but kindness for
you all – I love you , but hate Slavery , Now my dear Sir , will you
favor me by dropping me a line , telling me in what year I came to live
with you in Aliceanna st

Transcribe the excerpt from Frederick Douglas' letter:

of   your   dear   children .   They
☐☐   ☐☐☐☐   ☐☐☐☐   ☐☐☐☐☐☐☐☐   ☐☐☐☐

were   dear   to   me – and   are   still –
☐☐☐☐   ☐☐☐☐   ☐☐   ☐☐☐☐☐   ☐☐☐   ☐☐☐☐☐

indeed   I   feel   nothing   but
☐☐☐☐☐☐   ☐   ☐☐☐☐   ☐☐☐☐☐☐☐   ☐☐☐

kindness   for   you   all –   I   love
☐☐☐☐☐☐☐☐   ☐☐☐   ☐☐☐   ☐☐☐☐   ☐   ☐☐☐☐

you ,   but   hate   Slavery ,   Now   my
☐☐☐☐   ☐☐☐   ☐☐☐☐   ☐☐☐☐☐☐☐☐   ☐☐☐   ☐☐

dear   Sir ,   will   you   favor   me   by
☐☐☐☐   ☐☐☐☐   ☐☐☐☐   ☐☐☐   ☐☐☐☐☐   ☐☐   ☐☐

Transcribe the cursive letters:

dropping   *me*   *a*   *line,*   *telling*   *me*

in   *what*   *year*   *I*   *came*   *to*   *live*

with   *you*   *in*   *Aliceanna*   *st*

Copy in cursive the excerpt from Frederick Douglass letter.

_____

_____

_____

_____

_____

_____

_____

DECODING CURSIVE LEGEND

Aa	*Bb*	*Cc*	*Dd*	*Ee*	*Ff*	*Gg*	*Hh*	*Ii*	*Jj*	*Kk*	*Ll*	*Mm*
Aa	Bb	Cc	Dd	Ee	Ff	Gg	Hh	Ii	Jj	Kk	Ll	Mm
Nn	*Oo*	*Pp*	*Qq*	*Rr*	*Ss*	*Tt*	*Uu*	*Vv*	*Ww*	*Xx*	*Yy*	*Zz*
Nn	Oo	Pp	Qq	Rr	Ss	Tt	Uu	Vv	Ww	Xx	Yy	Zz

the year the Frigate was built by Mr. Beacham — The information is not for publication – and shall not be published — We are all hastening where all distinctions are ended, kindness to the humblest will not be unrewarded

the year the Frigate was built by Mr. Beacham The information is not for publication – and shall not be published. We are all hastening where all distinctions are ended, kindness to the humblest will not be unrewarded

Transcribe the cursive letters.

the   year   the   Frigate   was   built

by   Mr.   Beacham –   The

information   is   not   for

publication –   and   shall   not   be

published.   We   are   all   hastening

where   all   distinctions   are

Transcribe the cursive letters.

ended ,
☐☐☐☐☐

kindness
☐☐☐☐☐☐☐☐

to
☐☐

the
☐☐☐

humblest
☐☐☐☐☐☐☐☐

will
☐☐☐☐

not
☐☐☐

be
☐☐

unrewarded
☐☐☐☐☐☐☐☐☐☐

Copy in cursive the excerpt from Frederick Douglass letter.

_____

_____

_____

_____

_____

_____

_____

DECODING CURSIVE LEGEND

Aa	*Bb*	*Cc*	*Dd*	*Ee*	*Ff*	*Gg*	*Hh*	*Ii*	*Jj*	*Kk*	*Ll*	*Mm*
Aa	Bb	Cc	Dd	Ee	Ff	Gg	Hh	Ii	Jj	Kk	Ll	Mm
Nn	*Oo*	*Pp*	*Qq*	*Rr*	*Ss*	*Tt*	*Uu*	*Vv*	*Ww*	*Xx*	*Yy*	*Zz*
Nn	Oo	Pp	Qq	Rr	Ss	Tt	Uu	Vv	Ww	Xx	Yy	Zz

Perhaps you have heard that I have seen Miss Amanda that was, Mrs Sears that is, and was treated kindly such is the fact, Gladly would I see you and Mrs. Auld or Miss Sopha as I used to call her.

Perhaps you have heard that I have seen Miss Amanda that was, Mrs Sears that is, and was treated kindly such is the fact, Gladly would I see you and Mrs. Auld or Miss Sophia as I used to call her .

Transcribe the cursive letters.

Perhaps you have heard

that I have seen Miss

Amanda that was, Mrs Sears

that is, and was treated

kindly such is the fact,

Transcribe the cursive letters.

Gladly   *would*   *I*   *see*   *you*   *and*

Mrs.   *Auld*   *or*   *Miss*   *Sophia*

as   *I*   *used*   *to*   *call*   *her* .

Copy in cursive the excerpt from Frederick Douglass letter.

_____

_____

_____

_____

_____

_____

_____

DECODING CURSIVE LEGEND

Aa	Bb	Cc	Dd	Ee	Ff	Gg	Hh	Ii	Jj	Kk	Ll	Mm
Aa	Bb	Cc	Dd	Ee	Ff	Gg	Hh	Ii	Jj	Kk	Ll	Mm
Nn	Oo	Pp	Qq	Rr	Ss	Tt	Uu	Vv	Ww	Xx	Yy	Zz
Nn	Oo	Pp	Qq	Rr	Ss	Tt	Uu	Vv	Ww	Xx	Yy	Zz

I could have lived with you during life in freedom
though I ranaway from you so unceremoniously,
I did not know how soon I might be sold. But I hate
to talk about that. A line from you will find me Addressed Fred.K Douglass
Rochester N. York. I am dear sir very truly yours. Fred: Douglass

I could have lived with you during life i n freedom
though I ranaway from you so unceremoniously,
I did not know how soon I might be sold. But I hate
to talk about that. A line from you will find me Addressed Fred
K Douglass Rochester N. York . I am dear Sir very truly yours,
Fred Douglass

Transcribe the cursive of Frederick Douglas' letter.

I could have lived with you

□ ☐☐☐☐☐ ☐☐☐☐ ☐☐☐☐☐ ☐☐☐☐ ☐☐☐

during life in freedom though

☐☐☐☐☐☐ ☐☐☐☐ ☐☐ ☐☐☐☐☐☐☐ ☐☐☐☐☐☐

I ranaway from you so

□ ☐☐☐☐☐☐☐ ☐☐☐☐ ☐☐☐ ☐☐

unceremoniously I did not

☐☐☐☐☐☐☐☐☐☐☐☐☐☐☐ □ ☐☐☐ ☐☐☐

know how soon I might be sold .

☐☐☐☐ ☐☐☐ ☐☐☐☐ □ ☐☐☐☐☐ ☐☐ ☐☐☐☐

Transcribe the cursive letters.

But I hate to talk about that.

☐☐☐☐ ☐ ☐☐☐☐ ☐☐ ☐☐☐☐ ☐☐☐☐☐ ☐☐☐☐

A line from you will find me

☐ ☐☐☐☐ ☐☐☐☐ ☐☐☐ ☐☐☐☐ ☐☐☐☐ ☐☐

Addressed Fred K Douglass

☐☐☐☐☐☐☐☐☐ ☐☐☐☐ ☐ ☐☐☐☐☐☐☐☐

Rochester N. York. I am dear

☐☐☐☐☐☐☐☐☐ ☐ ☐☐☐☐ ☐ ☐☐ ☐☐☐☐

Sir very truly yours,

☐☐☐ ☐☐☐☐ ☐☐☐☐☐ ☐☐☐☐☐

Fred Douglass

☐☐☐☐ ☐☐☐☐☐☐☐☐

Copy in cursive the above excerpt from Frederick Douglass' letter.

_____

_____

_____

_____

_____

_____

_____

Rochester Oct. 4th (1857

Hugh Auld Esq
      My dear sir.

        My heart tells me that
you are too noble to treat with indifference the
request I am about to make, It is twenty years
Since I ranaway from you, or rather not from you
but from Slavery, and since then I have often felt
a Strong desire to hold a little correspondence with you
and to learn something of the position and prospects
of your dear children— They were dear to me— and
are Still— indeed I feel nothing but kindness for
you all— I love you, but hate Slavery, Now my
dear Sir, will you favor me by dropping me a line, telling
me in what year I came to live with you in Aliceanna st
the year the Frigate was built by Mr. Beacham—
The information is not for publication— and shall
not be published— We are all hastening where all
distinctions are ended, kindness to the humblest will
not be unrewarded
Perhaps you have heard that I have Seen Miss Amanda
that was, Mrs Sears that is, and was treated kindly
Such is the fact, Gladly would I See you and Mrs.
Auld— or Miss Sopha as I used to call her.
I could have lived with you during life in freedom
though I ranaway from you so unceremoniously,
I did not know how soon I might be sold, But I hate
to talk about that, A line from you will find me Addressed Fredk Douglass
Rochester N. York. I am dear sir very truly yours. Fred: Douglass

Read Frederick Douglass letter to his former owner, paying attention to spelling and grammar discrepancies that today would be considered errors. Write a cursive copy of the text by today's standards for proper English.

_____

_____

_____

_____

_____

_____

_____

_____

_____

_____

_____

_____

_____

_____

_____

_____

_____

_____

Write a letter to Frederick Douglass. Think about his life experiences. What questions would you like to ask him?

_____

_____

_____

_____

_____

_____

_____

_____

_____

_____

_____

_____

_____

_____

_____

_____

Primary Source

5.

Abraham Lincoln's
The Gettysburg Address
November 19, 1863

ABRAHAM LINCOLN'S GETTYSBURG ADDRESS, NOVEMBER 19, 1863

One of the most important Civil War battles, fought in early July of 1863 at Gettysburg, Pennsylvania, claimed the lives of 7000 American soldiers from the North and the South. Another 44000 were injured. Thousands of soldiers were buried at the sight of the battle. Despite the fierce and heroic efforts of the Confederate forces under General Lee, the Union forces won, and this battle became a turning point in the war.

Later that year, on November 19, Abraham Lincoln spoke at the official dedication of the Gettysburg Civil War Cemetery. His speech lasted only two minutes, yet inspired by the historical significance of this victory, his sentiments were moving and profound like no other in American history.

As he spoke, Lincoln presented the outcome of the Civil war as the test that would confirm or invalidate the great American experiment, a government of the people, by the people and for the people.

Today, we recognize the Gettysburg Address as one of the most powerful speeches in the English language. Historians worldwide agree that this is one of human history's greatest declarations of freedom and liberty. Not only is it important from a historical

Facsimile of Gettysburg address in Lincoln's hand on an envelope. Library of Congress

perspective, but it is just as relevant today. With so many people in America calling for social division, a return to segregation based on color and even the secession of states, one may wonder if a second civil war is in our future. Will there be another testing of the American experiment? Will our government of the people, by the people and for the people yet perish from this earth?

American archives have five copies of the Gettysburg speech. Some are working drafts, and others were copied later for posterity. We even have one kept in the Library of Congress, written on the back of an envelope:)

Today we focus on a clean version of John Hey's copy, often referred to as the second draft.

Four score and seven years ago our fathers brought forth on this continent, a new na- tion, conceived in Liberty, and dedicated to the proposition that all men are cre- ated equal.

Four score and seven years ago our fathers brought forth on this continent, a new na- tion, conceived in Liberty, and dedicated to the proposition that all men are cre- ated equal.

Transcribe the cursive text from the Gettysburg address.

Four score and seven years ago

our fathers brought forth on

this continent a new nation,

conceived in Liberty, and

Transcribe the cursive letters.

dedicated   to   the   proposition

that   all   men   are   created

equal.

Copy in cursive the first paragraph of the Gettysburg address.

_____

_____

_____

_____

_____

_____

_____

_____

_____

Now we are engaged in a great civil war,
testing whether that nation, or any nation
so conceived and so dedicated, can long
endure. We are met on a great battlefield
of that war. We have come to dedicate a

Now we are engaged in a great civil war,
testing whether that nation, or any nation
so conceived and so dedicated, can long
endure. We are met on a great battlefield
of that war. We have come to dedicate a

Transcribe the cursive text from the Gettysburg address.

Now we are engaged in a great

civil war, testing whether

that nation, or any nation so

Transcribe the cursive text from the Gettysburg address.

conceived and so dedicated

, can long endure. We are met

on a great battlefield of

that war. We have come to

dedicate a

Copy in cursive the excerpt from the Gettysburg address.

_____

_____

_____

_____

_____

_____

portion of that field, as a final resting place for those who here gave their lives, that that nation might live. It is alto. gether fitting and proper that we should do this.

portion of that field, as a final resting place for those who here gave their lives, that that nation might live. It is alto gether fitting and proper that we should do this.

Transcribe the cursive excerpt from the Gettysburg address.

portion   of   that   field,   as   a

final   resting   place   for   those

who   here   gave   their   lives

Transcribe the cursive letters.

that *that* *nation* *might* *live*

It is altogether fitting and

proper that we should do this.

Copy in cursive the above excerpt from the Gettysburg address.

But, in a larger sense, we can not dedicate— we can not consecrate— we can not
hallow— this ground. The brave men, living and dead, who struggled here, have consecrated it, far above our poor power to add

But, in a larger sense, we can not dedi-
cate- we can not consecrate- we can not
hallow - this ground. The brave men, living and dead, who struggled here, have consecrated it, far above our poor power to add

Transcribe the cursive text from the Gettysburg address.

But, in a larger sense, we can not

dedicate - we can not consecrate-

we can not hallow - this ground

Transcribe the cursive letters.

The brave men, living and

dead, who struggled here

have consecrated it, far

above our poor power to add

Copy in cursive the above excerpt from the Gettysburg address.

_____

_____

_____

_____

_____

_____

_____

or detract. The world will little note, nor long remember, what we say here, but it can never forget what they did here. It is for us the living, rather, to be dedicated here to

or detract. The world will little note, nor long remember, what we say here, but it can never forget what they did here. It is for us the living, rather, to be dedicated here to

Transcribe the cursive text from the Gettysburg address.

or detract. The world will

little note, nor long remember

what we say here, but it can

never forget what they did

Transcribe the cursive letters.

here. It is for us the living

rather, to be dedicated here to

Copy in cursive the above excerpt from the Gettysburg address.

the unfinished work which they who fought here have thus far so nobly advanced.
It is rather for us to be here dedicated to
the great task remaining before us- that
from these honored dead we take increased
devotion to that cause for which they gave

Transcribe the cursive text from the Gettysburg address.

the   unfinished   work   which   they

who   fought   here   have   thus   far

so   nobly   advanced.   It is   rather

Transcribe the cursive letters.

for us to be here dedicated

□□□ □□ □□ □□ □□□□ □□□□□□□□□

to the great task remaining

□□ □□□ □□□□□ □□□□ □□□□□□□□□

before us, that from these

□□□□□□ □□ □□□□ □□□□ □□□□□

honored dead we take increased

□□□□□□□ □□□□□ □□ □□□□ □□□□□□□□□

devotion to that cause for

□□□□□□□□ □□ □□□□ □□□□□ □□□

which they gave

□□□□□ □□□□ □□□□

Copy in cursive the above excerpt from the Gettysburg address.

_____

_____

_____

_____

_____

the last full measure of devotion - that
we here highly resolve that these dead shall
not have died in vain - that this nation,
under God, shall have a new birth of freedom, and that government of the people,

Transcribe the cursive text from the Gettysburg address.

the last full measure of
□□□ □□□□ □□□□ □□□□□□□ □□
devotion, that - we here highly
□□□□□□□□□ □□□□□ □□ □□□□ □□□□□□
resolve that these dead shall
□□□□□□□ □□□□ □□□□□ □□□□ □□□□□
not have died in vain - that this
□□□ □□□□ □□□□ □□ □□□□ □□□□ □□□□

Transcribe the cursive letters.

nation,   under God,   shall   have   a

new   birth   of   freedom, and   that

government   of   the   people,

Copy in cursive the above excerpt from the Gettysburg address.

by the people, for the people, shall not per-
ish from the earth.

Abraham Lincoln.

November 19. 1863.

by the people, for the people, shall not perish from the earth.

Abraham Lincoln

November 19 , 1863

Transcribe the cursive text from the Gettysburg address.

by the people, for the people,

shall not perish from the earth.

Abraham Lincoln

November 19, 1863

Copy in cursive the last excerpt from the Gettysburg address.

Do you have any questions for President Lincoln? Write him a note in cursive.

A Declaration by the Representatives of the UNITED STATES OF
AMERICA in General Congress assembled.

When in the course of human events it becomes necessary for one people to
dissolve the political bands which have connected them with another, and to assume
among the powers of the earth the separate and equal station to which the laws of na-
-ture & of nature's god entitle them, a decent respect to the opinions of mankind re-
-quires that they should declare the causes which impel them to the separation.

We hold these truths to be self evident; that all men are created equal; that
they are endowed by their Creator with inherent & inalienable rights; that among
these are life, liberty, & the pursuit of happiness; that to secure these rights, governments are instituted among men, deriving their just powers from the consent of the
governed; that whenever any form of government becomes destructive of these ends,
it is the right of the people to alter or to abolish it, and to institute new government,
laying it's foundation on such principles & organising it's powers in such form as to
them shall seem most likely to effect their safety & happiness. prudence indeed will
dictate that governments long established should not be changed for light & transient
causes. and accordingly all experience hath shewn that mankind are more disposed to
suffer while evils are sufferable, than ,   themselves by abolishing the forms
they are accustomed. but when a long train of abuses & usurpations, begun at a distin-
-guished period, & pursuing invariably the same object, evinces a design to reduce them
under absolute despotism, it is their right, it is their duty, to throw off such government
& to provide new guards for their future security. such has been the patient sufferance
of these colonies; & such is now the necessity which constrains them to expunge their
former systems of government. the history of the present king of Great Britain, is a
history of unremitting injuries & usurpations, among which appears no solitary fact
to contradict the uniform tenor of the rest; but all have in direct object the esta-
-blishment of an absolute tyranny over these states. to prove this let facts be sub-
-mitted to a candid world, for the truth of which we pledge a faith yet unsullied by falsehood.
He has refused his assent to laws the most wholesome & necessary for the public good.
he has forbidden his governors to pass laws of immediate & pressing importance, un-
-less suspended in their operation till his assent should be obtained; & when so
suspended, he has neglected utterly to attend to them:
he has refused to pass other laws for the accomodation of large districts of people, unless
those people would relinquish the right of representation in the legislature,
a right inestimable to them & formidable to tyrants only:

Bonus exercise:

Examine the document on the previous page. Do you recognize this text? Name the document. Read it and write a copy of the text in cursive. Just like a real historian/archeologist, you might need to use a magnifying glass to see better.

_____

_____

_____

_____

_____

_____

_____

_____

_____

_____

_____

_____

_____

_____

_____

_____

Write a letter to your future self. In your own words, describe today's world. Record a few facts about your life, such as who are your family members? Note their names, ages, and what they like to do for fun? What do they talk about at the dinner table? Who is the President today? Are there any wars America is involved in? What is the price for a gallon of milk? What do you think your job is going to be in 20 years?

LETTER TO MYSELF

_____
place

_____
date

_____
_____
_____
_____
_____
_____
_____
_____
_____
_____
_____
_____
_____
_____
_____
_____
_____
_____

Please, Leave us a Quick Review!

If you found Learning Patriot's Cursive Workbook helpful, please leave a review on Amazon. Your feedback will help other parents to find this book and make informed decisions. Thank you for your support!

>> Scan QR code to find the Amazon Review Page

CHECK BOOK 2 OF THE LEARNING PATRIOT'S COLLECTION

Reading and Writing with the Bill of Rights

A fun and engaging way for kids to learn cursive writing while exploring one of the most important documents in American history. The Bill of Rights is a foundational document that outlines the fundamental rights and freedoms of every citizen in the United States. By learning how to read and write in cursive, kids will be able to read and analyze the original text, gaining a deeper understanding of the history and meaning behind these important rights.

In **Reading and Writing with the Bill of Rights** kids will enjoy a variety of puzzles and games designed to make learning cursive fun and engaging. By practicing their writing skills, they will be able to read and analyze primary sources, such as historical documents, letters, and diaries. In today's world of digital communication, it is more important than ever to teach kids the value of reading and writing in cursive. Give your child the gift of history and critical thinking skills with **Reading and Writing with the Bill of Rights**.

Scan the QR code to Order on Amazon now   >>

COMING SOON

Learning Patriot's Handbook for Logic

This book teaches kids how to think logically and detect logical errors in everyday life. In today's Western culture, children are being taught all about emotions and sensitivity, but the importance of critical thinking and common sense is often overlooked. With this book, children will learn how to approach problems with a clear and analytical mind, developing the skills needed to make informed decisions and avoid common pitfalls.

The **Learning Patriot's Handbook for Logic** is an essential tool for the next generation, as critical thinking skills become increasingly important in today's rapidly changing world. With fun exercises and relatable examples, kids will learn how to identify and evaluate arguments, understand logical fallacies, and develop their own informed opinions. By teaching children how to think logically, this book will help them become independent thinkers who are equipped to navigate complex issues and make sound decisions. Don't let your child fall behind in today's fast-paced world - give them the gift of critical thinking with the **Learning Patriot's Handbook For Logic.**

References

Franklin, Benjamin. Benjamin Franklin Papers: Series I, -1783; Petition of the Continental Congress to the King, Philadelphia, Pa., 1774, Oct. 26 vol. 10. 1774. Manuscript/Mixed Material. https://www.loc.gov/item/mss21451011/.

Washington, George. George Washington Papers, Series 2, Letterbooks -1799: Letterbook 24, April 3, 1793 - March 3, 1797. 1793. Manuscript/Mixed Material. https://www.loc.gov/item/mgw2.024/.

Thomas Jefferson to Danbury, Connecticut, Baptist Association, January 1, with Copy. -01-01, 1802. Manuscript/Mixed Material. https://www.loc.gov/item/mtjbib010955/.
Douglass, Jefferson, Frederick Douglass to hisHugh Auld, October 4, 185, https://www.gilderlehrman.org/news/frederick-douglass-writes-his-former-owner-day-1857

Lincoln, Abraham. Facsimile of Gettysburg address in Lincoln's hand on an envelope. Commercial letter, Inc., St. Louis, Missouri, n. d. Manuscript/Mixed Material. https://www.loc.gov/item/scsm000717/.

Douglass, Frederick. "I Love You But I Hate Slavery." Gilder Lehrman Institute of American History, 27 Dec. 2022, www.gilderlehrman.org/history-resources/spotlight-primary-source/i-love-you-hate-slavery-frederick-douglass-his-former. Accessed 27 Dec. 2022.

Emmet, Thomas Addis Collector. "Declaration of Independance." NYPL's Domain Archive, 1757, nypl.getarchive.net/media/document-fair-copy-of-the-declaration-of-independence-03ec5b.

You can find many more manuscripts, personal letters and other primary sources on the Library of Congress' website at https://www.loc.gov/.

Don't hesitate to study like a real historian. You may have heard that "History is written by the victors". True statement. What's also true is that often one man's truth is another man's misinformation. The best way to know what really happened is to do your own research, read the primary sources, and judge for yourself.

Certificate of Completion

Proudly Awarded To

_____

your name here

For Successfully Completing The Bill Of Rights And Cursive Proficiency

_____

your signature here

Made in the USA
Middletown, DE
07 June 2025

76692639R00097